CW00392184

Text: *Carl Rogers*

Photographs: *Carl Rogers, Shutterstock, Tony Bowerman*

Design: *Carl Rogers*

ISBN 978-1-902512-27-3

A CIP catalogue record for this book is available from the British Library

Top 10 Walks series created by
Northern Eye Books

n Northern
  Eye

www.northerneyebooks.co.uk
www.top10walks.co.uk

Cover: *Descending the northeast ridge of Y Garn.* **Photo: Carl Rogers**

Warning!

Walking and scrambling on the mountains can be dangerous and carries the risk of personal injury or death. Do not attempt these walks unless you have suitable experience or training. Conditions can change rapidly, particularly on the high fells, and it is important that walkers have the ability to assess both the conditions and the associated risks.

Important Advice: The routes described in this book are undertaken at the reader's own risk. Walkers should take into account their level of fitness, wear suitable footwear and clothing, and carry food and water. It is also advisable to take the relevant OS map with you in case you get lost and leave the area covered by our maps.

Whilst every care has been taken to ensure the accuracy of the route directions, the publishers cannot accept responsibility for errors or omissions, or for changes in the details given. Nor can the publisher and copyright owners accept responsibility for any consequences arising from the use of this book.

If you find any inaccuracies in either the text or maps, please write or email us at the address below. Thank you.

First published under licence from Northern Eye Books in 2014 by : **Mara Books**
22 Crosland Terrace, Helsby, Cheshire WA6 9LY
Email: carl@marabooks.co.uk

For sales enquiries, please call 01928 723 744

Twitter: @CarlMarabooks
          @Northerneyeboo
          @Top10walks

Contents

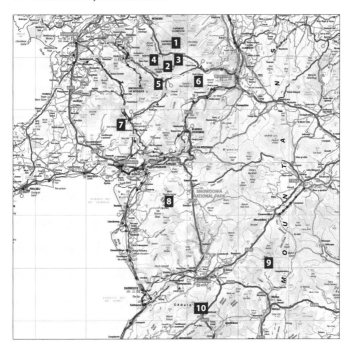

Snowdonia National Park

Snowdonia is one of the most celebrated and spectacular highland areas in the British Isles — a region of hills, lakes, mountains and wild moorland occupying the northwest corner of Wales.

Snowdonia National Park (Parc Cenedlaethol Eryri) was established in 1951 as the third National Park in Britain, following the Peak District and the Lake District. It covers 827 square miles (2,140 square kilometres) and, rather surprisingly, has 37 miles (60 kilometres) of coastline. There is great variety within this small area — the park contains all of Wales' 14 highest mountains, as well as a host of lakes, woods, beautiful valleys and high moorland.

The unique flora and fauna of the area includes rare mammals such as otter, polecat and feral goat. Birds of prey include peregrine, osprey, merlin and red kite, with rare plants like the Arctic-alpine Snowdon lily and the unique Snowdon hawkweed.

Snowdonia's mountains

The hills and mountains of this region will captivate any lover of wild mountain scenery, with around 100 summits above 2,000 feet (approximately 610 metres). Fourteen of these exceed 3,000 feet (914 metres), of which four raise their heads above 1,000 metres.

The highest and most spectacular peaks are in the north around Snowdon where all the fourteen 3,000-foot summits are to be found. Rocky ridges, high crags and one or two sharp, Alpine-like summits make this area the best known, with by far the most visitors. In the south the hills are lower, softer, less rocky and generally far less busy. So for drama and stature head north, for softer skylines and solitude head south.

"Only a hill; but all of life to me,
up there between the sunset and the sea"

Geoffrey Winthrop Young, *poet and mountaineer (1876–1958)*

A 'sea' of cloud fills Cwm Dyli on Snowdon

TOP 10 **Walks:** Mountain Walks

With over 100 high summits in Snowdonia how do you choose a top ten? The following walks have been chosen to give a variety of routes, spread across the entire National Park, with most of the main hill groups represented. For each mountain the most scenic route has been chosen and where possible these are well-established, classic paths, easy to follow, with good access and official parking. Enjoy Snowdonia.

The high Carneddau — page 8

The Glyderau — page 14

Tryfan — page 20

Y Garn & Devil's Kitchen — page 26

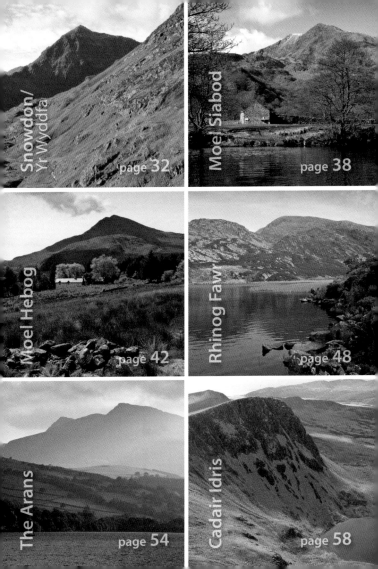

Carnedd Llewelyn rises above the Ogwen valley

The high **Carneddau**

*Glan Denna – Afon Lloer – Pen yr Ole Wen – Carnedd
Dafydd – Carnedd Llewelyn – Yr Elen – Pen yr Helgi Du*

Distance/time: 19km/11¾ miles

Start: There is ample free parking at the eastern end of Llyn Ogwen on the A5 between Glan Dena and Gwern Gof Uchaf farm

Grid ref: SH 668 606

Summits: Pen-yr Ole Wen, Carnedd Dafydd, Carnedd Llewelyn, & Pen yr Helgi Du. Yr Elen optional

Ordnance Survey Map: Ordnance Survey Outdoor Leisure OL17 *Snowdon/Yr Wyddfa – Conwy Valley/Dyffryn Conwy*

Walk outline

A steady ascent and a short, easy scramble to Pen-yr Ole Wen is followed by an elevated ridge walk over three high summits with wide views south to the Glyderau and Tryfan. Descent is by Carnedd Llewelyn's long southeast ridge, across the narrow Bwlch Eryl Farchog to Pen yr Helgi Du and then by the gentle ridge of Y Braich with superb views.

The high Carneddau

The Carneddau are Snowdonia's northern-most mountain group — a high, bulky plateauland containing the greatest extent of high ground in the whole of Wales and almost half of Snowdonia's elite 3,000-foot summits. The Carneddau are broad, stocky mountains having height and stature, but lacking the graceful outlines of their better known neighbours. As a result they are the least busy of Snowdonia's high mountains.

Yr Elen

This route uses the most popular access to the high tops from Ogwen. Once the climbing is done, you can cruise along the fine, elevated ridge between Carnedd Dafydd and Carnedd Llewelyn with minimal effort. Views are superb.

Keep an eye out for the semi-wild Welsh mountain ponies which graze the northern Carneddau.

Welsh mountain pony

The Walk

1. From the **A5** at the eastern end of **Llyn Ogwen**, cross the bridge and follow the track past the house 'Glan Dena', situated in a small conifer wood. Continue along the track towards 'Tal y Llyn Ogwen' farm, but turn right up to a stile in the wall immediately before the farm. After the stile, the path curves right to follow **Afon Lloer**. Cross the stream higher up and follow it until the angle eases as you approach **Cwm Lloer**.

2. Head left before you reach the lake to begin the ascent of **Pen-yr**

© Crown copyright and database rights 2014. Ordnance Survey. Licence number 100022856

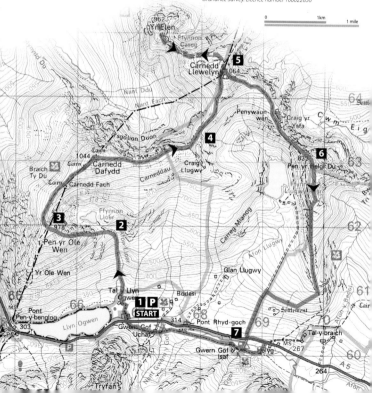

Island prospect: *Looking down the wide sweep of Cwm Llafar towards Anglesey*

Ole Wen's east ridge. A broken rock spur is negotiated by a short easy gully scramble to gain a well-defined path that keeps close to the crags overlooking the south wall of Cwm Lloer to the right.

Pen-yr Ole Wen is the perfect viewpoint for the magnificent hollow of Cwm Idwal, enclosed by Glyder Fawr and Y Garn, and is well worth the short detour to the top of the southwest ridge.

3. From **Pen-yr Ole Wen** a good path heads northeast along the ridge to **Carnedd Dafydd** (about 1.5 kilometres/1 mile away). From Carnedd Dafydd the path continues along the broad ridge above the huge cliffs known as the 'Black Ladders' (Ysgolion Duon).

4. A short drop to **Bwlch Cyfryw-drum** (The Saddle) is followed by a steady ascent over scree to **Carnedd Llewelyn**, Snowdonia's third highest mountain and the highest point in the Carneddau.

(If you want to include the summit of Yr Elen it is a straightforward 3 kilometre/2 mile out-and-back detour along the northwest ridge.)

Final summit: *On Bwlch Eryl Farchog with the final summit, Pen yr Helgi Du, ahead and the shimmering waters of Ffynnon Llugwy below, in stunning winter conditions*

5. From Carnedd Llewelyn follow the broad east ridge with the deep glacial trough of Cwm Eigiau ahead. The ridge is steep at first, then more gentle and grassy until you reach the rim of **Craig yr Ysfa** and its famous 'Amphitheatre'. The ridge narrows now and there is a little scrambling to reach **Bwlch Eryl Farchog**. (You could shorten the walk here if needed by taking the path which zig-zags down to the lake and following the reservoir road down to the A5.) A

short scramble from the bwlch leads to **Pen yr Helgi Du**, another superb viewpoint, particularly for Tryfan seen dramatically across the valley.

6. From here, head due south along the gentle, rounded ridge of **Y Braich** (*'the arm'*). Almost at the bottom of the ridge, pass through a gap in a crossing wall and bear right over open ground to cross a leat by a footbridge. This feeds water into the nearby Llyn Cowlyd Reservoir. Turn right now and follow the **leat** to the reservoir access road leading to up Ffynnon Llugwy. Turn left down the road to the A5.

7. To avoid the 2 kilometres/1¼ miles

or so back along the A5, turn left along the road and just before a small conifer wood, go right over the stile and make your way through a boulder-strewn field to a group of old pines. The stile here leads onto a bridleway, once the main road through the valley. Turn right and follow the path back past **Gwern Gof Uchaf** farm to reach the A5 and complete the walk. ♦

Last independent Welsh princes

The two highest summits in the Carneddau are said to be named after Llywelyn ap Gruffudd, the last independent prince of Wales, and his rival brother Dafydd ap Gruffudd. Alternatively, they could be named after Llywelyn the Great, and his son Dafydd ap Llywelyn. Either way there is little doubt that these mountains carry the names of eminent Welsh princes who lived and ruled in their shadow.

Glyder Fach from Llyn Bochlwyd

The **Glyderau**

*Llyn Ogwen – Llyn Bochlwyd – Bwlch Tryfan – Glyder Fach –
Castell y Gwynt – Glyder Fawr – Devil's Kitchen – Llyn Idwal*

Distance/time: 9.75km/6 miles

Start: Parking is available at the western end of Llyn Ogwen
on the A5 and in lay-bys along the lake. Start the walk from the
refreshment kiosk at the western end of the lake.

Grid ref: SH 649 604

Summits: Glyder Fach & Glyder Fawr

Ordnance Survey Map: Ordnance Survey Outdoor Leisure OL17
Snowdon/Yr Wyddfa – Conwy Valley/Dyffryn Conwy

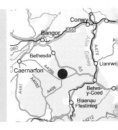

Walk outline

*A good footpath takes you via the high mountain hollow of Cwm
Bochlwyd to Bwlch Tryfan and up onto the Glyder plateau by the
mountain's rounded eastern shoulder. Almost level walking across
the plateau between the two summits gives superb views and
allows the walker to enjoy the unusual rock architecture. Descent is
by the famous Devil's Kitchen and Cwm Idwal where the fine rock
scenery continues.*

The Glyderau

The two giants of the Glyder range stand shoulder to shoulder,
separated by a wasteland of shattered rocks and tottering
spikes, giving the summit plateau a lunar-like quality. To the
south the land falls away to Dyffryn Mymbyr and the Llanberis
Pass, but to the north things are very different — a landscape
of deep glacial cwms separated by fine rock arêtes. These peaks
are second only to Snowdon in their rugged grandeur.

Llyn Idwal

Approaching from the north, this route avoids a direct frontal
assault on the mountain, but still samples some of its fine rock
scenery. You may see the rare dotterel on the high summit
plateau. This hardy little bird thrives in the harsh, tundra-like
environment of the highest tops.

Dotterel

The Walk

1. Take the well-constructed footpath which leaves the car park beside the little **snack bar**. Where this turns right in about 400 metres to Cwm Idwal, keep ahead on a narrower path, soon rising more steeply beside the stream to reach the hanging valley of **Cwm Bochlwyd** with is sheltered lake.

2. Stay with the path which continues ahead above the northeastern shore of the lake to **Bwlch Tryfan**. Cross the

stone wall which straddles the saddle and continue on the footpath ahead across scree to gain Glyder Fach's broad east ridge.

3. Once you have gained the ridge turn sharp right up the final slopes — a mix of grass and jumbled rocks — to **the summit**.

The summit of Glyder Fach is flat but far from unremarkable. Views southwest to Snowdon and north to Llyn Ogwen and Tryfan are superb and the summit plateau, with its chaotic rocks, can seem quite 'other worldly' particularly in misty

Bizarre summit: *A walker stands on the curious rock table know as The Cantilever*

conditions. The highest point — which can sometimes be difficult to decide on — lies just to the west of the famous rock table known as 'The Cantilever'.

4. Continue west across the plateau to the equally famous **Castell y Gwynt** — 'Castle of the Winds' — a group of rock spikes 'as romantic as their name'. The prospect of Snowdon with Castell y Gwynt in the foreground is one of Snowdonia's classic sights. The path skirts the rocks to the south (left) to

regain the ridge where it narrows at **Bwlch y Ddwy Glyder** and there is a view down into Cwm Bochlwyd and across to Tryfan. (From here a path rises to the right along the rim of Cwm Bochlwyd to the top of the rock ridge of Y Gribin which could be used to shorten the route if needed [scrambling].)

The path ahead continues to **Glyder Fawr** whose summit, like Glyder Fach, is marked by groups of jumbled rock formations providing mysterious foregrounds for views of the Snowdon group.

Shadowy cwms: *Glyder Fach (l) and Glyder Fawr (r) and the sheltered valleys of Cwm Bochlwyd and Cwm Idwal*

5. The usual descent from Glyder Fawr is by a well-worn scree path, which heads northwest and is marked regularly by cairns. In its lower reaches this is very loose and leads to the broad bwlch above the **Devil's Kitchen** where it joins the Cwm Idwal–Nant Peris path beside **Llyn y Cŵn**.

6. Turn right by the lake and follow the well constructed path steeply down beside the Devil's Kitchen into **Cwm Idwal**.

Lower down a short detour to the left will take you to the bottom of the 'Kitchen' itself.

7. Below the Devils' Kitchen the path makes its way through a jumble of massive boulders. A fork in the path partway through the **boulder field** marks the divide between the paths which run along the eastern and western shores of **Llyn Idwal**. Take your pick here; both options are similar in length and terrain. The right-hand option will take you below the impressive rock face known as the **Idwal Slabs** returning along a formalised stone-faced path to Llyn Ogwen. The

left-hand option offers the best views back into the cwm across the lake.

For the latter route, bear left at the fork and follow the path down through the boulders and along the eastern shore of Llyn Idwal. At the end of the lake go right, along the shingle beach, and cross the footbridge over the outflow. Turn left and follow the well-made footpath back to the car park. ◆

Exotic rocks

The summit of Glyder Fach contains some of the most unusual rock formations in Snowdonia. The most famous is probably the 'Cantilever Stone', a table-like formation almost on the highest point, whilst the group of shattered rocks known as Castell y Gwynt lies a little to the west and makes an unrivalled foreground to the view of Snowdon. Both were featured in Walt Disney's 1981 movie Dragonslayer.

Tryfan and Little Tyrfan seen from Gwern Gof Uchaf

Tryfan

Gwern Gof Uchaf – Little Tryfan – Heather Terrace – South Ridge – Adam & Eve – Bwlch Tryfan – Braich y Ddeugwm

Distance/time: 8km / 5 miles.

Start: There is a lay-by on the A5 at the eastern end of Llyn Ogwen between the lake and the track to Gwern Gof Uchaf farm

Grid ref: SH 671 605

Summits: Tryfan

Ordnance Survey Map: Ordnance Survey Outdoor Leisure OL17 *Snowdon/Yr Wyddfa – Conwy Valley/Dyffryn Conwy*

Walk outline

Rough, steep walking on the lower slopes of the mountain to reach Heather Terrace. This takes an bold line across the massive East Face of the mountain. Rock scenery is impressive for much of the ascent. There is a little scrambling with just one short section near the summit where there is some unavoidable exposure. Return is by the long grassy ridge of Braich y Ddeugwm with great views.

Little Tryfan

Tryfan

This superb rock peak is often considered to be off-limits to anyone not prepared to use their hands as well as their feet to reach its summit. But by the easiest route (South Ridge) there are just one or two places where you will need to take your hands out of your pockets. Care is still needed however, particularly in descent, and the mountain's airy summit may not be to everyone's liking!

This route uses Heather Terrace — the distinctive rake which runs below the East Face of the mountain — to reach the South Ridge. The delightful grassy ridge of Braich y Ddeugwm, with its spectacular views of Tryfan, is used to complete the route. Tryfan is an ideal place to see and hear ravens with their distinctive 'croaking' call.

Raven

The Walk

1. Walk east along the **A5** and turn right down the track to **Gwern Gof Uchaf farm**. Follow the track to the farm passing it on the left-hand side where a stile leads over the wall onto a bridleway. Turn right along the bridleway for a few metres to a point level with the farm outbuildings and bear left on a footpath which heads towards Tryfan.

Ignore a left turn at a fork in the path continuing ahead, to reach the prominent rock slab known as '**Little Tryfan**' where you will often see rock climbers. Walk up beside the slab and keep a look out for the path which soon bears right up over small rock ribs to reach a fence.. Don't cross the nearby stile, instead, take the path to the right and walk up parallel to the fence. Higher up the path rises by **stone steps through a short gully**.

2. At the top of the gully take the path immediately on the left which leads onto **Heather Terrace**.

Airy summit: *Tryfan has one of the rockiest summits in Snowdonia with impressive views and big drops on all sides*

NB. Give yourself a little time to locate the correct path here. The terrace is nowhere near as well defined when you are on it as it looks from the valley, particularly at the start. The correct path bears left as soon as you reach the top of the gully. It is well used and can be followed comfortably. The rock scenery is also superb as you pass below the impressive buttresses of the East Face high above the valley below.

3. At the end of **Heather Terrace**, turn right up a broad, short scree slope onto the **South Ridge** of the mountain. Cross the stile over the wall and follow the path rightwards up the broad rocky ridge to the **summit** marked by the twin rocks of '**Adam and Eve**'.

The summit of Tryfan is a remarkable place — one of only two true rock summits in the whole of Snowdonia. The views are magnificent and the situation exposed, with the spectacular fall into Cwm Tryfan just beyond Adam & Eve a dizzying 600 metres!

Mountain vista: *A panorama showing the spectacular East Face of Tryfan and the equally rocky Bristly Ridge on Glyder Fach rising above the wilds of Cwm Tryfan*

4. Retrace your ascent route down the **South Ridge** passing the **South Peak** over to the left to the small saddle where the route from Heather Terrace reached the ridge. Ignore this (unless you want to retrace your ascent route) continuing down the broad rocky ridge to **Bwlch Tryfan** — the saddle between Tryfan and Glyder Fach — where there is another wall.

5. Ahead rise the rocks of Bristly Ridge and the northern cliffs of Glyder Fach.

The '**Miners' Track**', a path linking the mines on Snowdon with Bethesda, crosses the saddle here at its lowest point and continues across the screes to the left to reach the rounded shoulder of Glyder Fach. Follow this path left over the wall and across to the shoulder.

6. Once on the skyline, bear left to the scattering of small lakes (**Llyn Caseg-fraith**) to locate the top of **Braich y Ddeugwm** — the long finger-like ridge forming the eastern side of Cwm Tryfan.

There is a footpath here but it is faint and could be very difficult to find in poor visibility. In good visibility no path is needed — once on the ridge the

walking is a delight with springy turf underfoot and stunning views of Tryfan and your route across Heather Terrace.

7. The ridge ends above **Gwern Gof Isaf** farm. Walk past the farm and down the access track towards the road. Just before the bridge turn left along the bridleway which follows the line of the old road back to **Gwern Gof Uchaf** farm to complete the route. ♦

Adam and Eve

Early stagecoach travellers are said to have 'gasped in awe' and 'shielded their eyes in terror' (as was the fashion of the day) as they passed below Tryfan's huge east face. Others voiced heartfelt concern for the sanity of the two tiny figures they could see trembling on its topmost rocks. Here, of course, they were mistaken: the two 'tiny figures' are actually two curious rock pillars — 'Adam and Eve' — the highest point on the mountain.

Y Garn, the 'Armchair Mountain' seen from the summit of Tryfan

Y Garn & Devil's Kitchen

Llyn Ogwen – Llyn Idwal – Devil's Kitchen – Llyn y Cŵn – Y Garn – Northeast ridge – Llyn Clyd – Idwal Cottage

Distance/time: 7.5km/4¾ miles

Start: Parking is available at the western end of Llyn Ogwen and in laybys along the lake. Start the walk from the refreshment kiosk

Grid ref: SH 650 604

Summits: Y Garn

Ordnance Survey Map: Ordnance Survey Outdoor Leisure OL17 *Snowdon/Yr Wyddfa – Conwy Valley/Dyffryn Conwy*

Walk outline

An easy walk along a well constructed path to Cwm Idwal with its beautiful lake and spectacular rock scenery. This is followed by a steep climb on a good path through a huge boulder field to the sinister gorge of the Devil's Kitchen. A shattered terrace leads to easier ground and a long gradual climb takes you to the summit of Y Garn. Descent is by the steep northeast ridge with superb views.

Y Garn and the Devil's Kitchen

Sometimes referred to as the 'Armchair Mountain', from the two enclosing ridges which embrace the tiny Llyn Clyd, Y Garn dominates the view west along Llyn Ogwen. Of the two ridges only the northeast ridge provides a walkable route, but it is mercilessly steep.

Descending from Y Garn

This route takes a more leisurely approach to the mountain via the beautiful and impressive amphitheatre of Cwm Idwal — worthy of a visit in its own right — and the famous cleft known as the 'Devil's Kitchen' (Twll Du). The steep northeast ridge — which gives stunning views into the Ogwen valley — is used as a descent. You may see the carnivorous sundew plant around the shores of Llyn Idwal. It uses tiny leaves to catch and digest small insects.

Sundew

The Walk

1. Take the well constructed footpath which leaves the car park beside the little snack bar and toilet block. For the first 400 metres the path heads southwest towards Tryfan, before curving right towards **Cwm Idwal**.

2. At **Llyn Idwal** there are paths along each side of the lake — both lead to the head of the lake below the **Devil's Kitchen**.

The path along the **left-hand shore** leads up below the clean sweep of rock known as the **Idwal slabs**. The path passes directly below the slabs which are often dotted with rock climbers.

From here a stone-faced footpath veers right up the huge boulder field towards the dripping rocks of the famous **Devil's Kitchen**. (Continue from point 3.)

The option along the **right-hand shore** or far side of the lake is a little longer but has slightly better views (yes, hard to imagine but they do get better!)

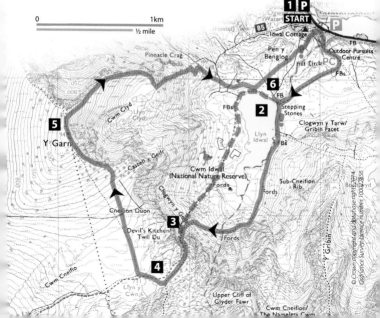

Grand prospect: *The stunning view of the Ogwen valley and Tryfan from Y Garn's northeast ridge*

For this option, bear right as soon as you reach the lake, over the footbridge and then along a lovely shingle 'beach'.

This is a superb spot, a great place to linger and enjoy the stunning surroundings and worth remembering if you have plenty of time on the descent.

At the end of the beach go through the gate and follow the obvious path that swings leftwards above the shore.

The mounds you pass here are the eroded remains of glacial moraines left behind by the small glacier that once filled the valley. Moraines such as this act as a kind of 'footprint' giving us an impression of the area covered by the final permanent ice before its retreat.

At the end of the lake the path steepens as it begins to climb towards the huge boulder field that lies immediately below the Devil's Kitchen.

3. Both paths meet just below the gorge and continue the climb soon swinging left-wards along a shattered terrace to

Mountain amphitheatre: *Llyn Idwal is enclosed on three sides by huge rock walls*

reach **Llyn y Cŵn** ('lake of the dogs'), on the broad ridge.

This is another great place to take a break with an easy climb ahead and great views to Snowdon and back down to Llyn Idwal.

4. From the lake, bear right up the broad easy-angled slopes which rise to **Y Garn**. As you near the shoulder of the mountain, the path follows the edge of the **Cwm Clyd** with its tiny mountain pool to reach the **summit**.

The views from Y Garn are grand on all sides, but it will most likely be the prospect of Llyn Idwal and Llyn Ogwen several hundred metres below and the serrated profile of Tryfan that will captivate you.

5. To descend, walk north along the ridge until a footpath can be seen dropping steeply down the **northeast ridge**. The path is quite steep and loose in places but easily followed. It requires extreme care in icy conditions.

At about the halfway point the angle eases and you have a view to **Llyn Clyd** on your right. Continue down the ridge which steepens again before reaching the shore of **Llyn Idwal**.

6. Return can be made by the outgoing route from the end of the lake, but a better option is to look for a path which heads left about halfway along the lake to a stile in the fence. Cross the stile and follow the path ahead over grass to cross a second stile which leads down into a small man-made gorge to emerge in the car park to complete the route. ♦

Cwm Idwal and the Devil's Kitchen

Known as the Devil's Kitchen, the dark chasm in the rock wall at the head of Cwm Idwal earned its name from the mist which rises up through the centre of the cliff face. This unique mountain valley was formed by glaciation and supports a host of rare and fragile flora, including Arctic-alpine plants. These include the Snowdon lily, mountain avens, and many members of the saxifrage family.

Crib Goch rises above Bwlch Moch with Snowdon beyond

Snowdon/Yr Wyddfa

Pen-y-pass – Bwlch Moch – Zig-zags – Bwlch Glas – Snowdon – Zig-zags – Glaslyn – Llyn Llydaw

Distance/time: 12km/7½ miles

Start: There is a moderate sized car park at Pen-y-Pass (often full). Alternatives at Pen-y-Gwyrd or Nant Peris Park & Ride. Fees payable

Grid ref: Pen-y-Pass SH 647 557; Peny-y-Gwyryd SH 659 557; Park & Ride SH 607 583

Summits: Snowdon (Yr Wyddfa)

Ordnance Survey Map: Ordnance Survey Outdoor Leisure OL17 *Snowdon/Yr Wyddfa – Conwy Valley/Dyffryn Conwy*

Walk outline

A gradual climb along a rocky, well constructed path leads to Bwlch Moch. From here you enter the Snowdon Horseshoe with its grand scenery. Old mine workings add extra interest, before the final climb up the famous 'Zig-zags' to join the Snowdon Mountain Railway and the Llanberis Path, which is followed to the summit. Descent is by a return down the 'Zig-zags' and a steep rocky path to Glaslyn and Llyn Llydaw. The remains of an old mining road are used to return to Pen-y-Pass.

Snowdon/Yr Wyddfa

From any approach Snowdon demands attention — its height, architectural complexity and dramatic skylines dominate the whole of northern Snowdonia. Even the height and closeness of its neighbours takes nothing away from this great mountain. If you were to place it amongst the giants of the Scottish Higlands it would still stand proud and aloof.

As far as routes to the summit are concerned, you are spoilt for choice — but the most impressive of the classic paths is from Pen-y-Pass and leads up through Cwm Dyli. Keep a look out for peregrines. They nest in the high, inaccessible cliff faces of the mountains.

Bwlch Glas

Peregrines

Sea of cloud: *Stunning conditions on Snowdon's summit*

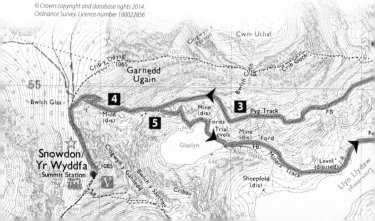

The Walk

A path below the road links the parking area at Pen-y-Gwryd with Pen-y-pass.

1. From the **Pen-y-Pass** car park the obvious exit from the lower car park is the Miners' Track (return route). However the best ascent is via the **Pyg Track** which exits from the higher car park just behind the **café** ('Gorphwysfa Restaurant') through a **gap in the stone wall** and under power lines.

Follow the Pyg Track — a well constructed path with views down the Llanberis Pass and ahead to the shapely, pyramidal summit of Crib Goch to **Bwlch Moch**, the saddle on the ridge and the point at which you enter the Snowdon Horseshoe (about 1.5 kilometres).

From Bwlch Moch there are superb views down to Llyn Llydaw and its causeway, and beyond to the 300-metre face of Y Lliwedd. Ahead is Snowdon looking deceptively close. To the right here is the steep path leading up to Crib Goch, but the Pyg Track continues over the stiles ahead to contour along the mountain's southern slopes.

2. Following the Pyg Track you eventually reach a superb viewpoint where Glaslyn (lake) and the dramatic summit cone of Snowdon can be seen to perfection rising above the lake.

Continue on the contouring path to an even closer viewpoint directly above Glaslyn.

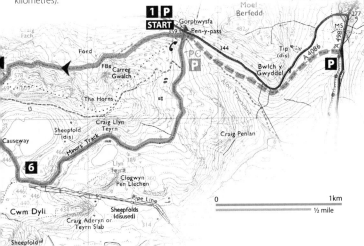

Roof of Wales: *The view from Bwlch Glas into Cwm Dyli with Snowdon on the right*

3. From here the path curves around the cwm passing the **junction with the Miners' Track** which comes up from the left (marked by an upright stone — take note of this for the descent).

4. Higher up you reach the foot of the famous 'Zig-zags' which negotiate the final steep slopes to **Bwlch Glas**.

The Bwlch Glas is marked by a **2-metre upright stone pillar** and it is here you meet with the Llanberis Path and the **Snowdon Mountain Railway**.

Turn left for the final ten-minute walk to the summit.

To descend, return to the upright stone on Bwlch Glas and descend the 'Zig-zags'. As the angle eases the path swings leftwards taking a more gradual traversing line with mining remains below.

5. Look for the junction with the **Miners' Track** noted on the ascent and marked by an **upright stone pillar**. This path descends down a wide scree gully to the shore of **Glaslyn**. (Avoid a path which breaks away slightly earlier and takes a more diagonal line passing close to mines before reaching the lake.)

Follow the path along the shore of Glaslyn to the outflow, then descend beside the stream to **Llyn Llydaw**. Continue along the northern shore of the lake and across the **stone causeway** originally built by miners working in the **Glaslyn Mines** during the nineteenth century.

6. Beyond the causeway the path is virtually level and wide — almost a road — and contours the slopes back to Pen-y-Pass to complete the walk. ♦

Summit buildings

There have been buildings on the summit of Snowdon since at least the early nineteenth century. These catered for visitors who climbed to the summit on pony to view the sunrise. The 'hotel' was little more than a wooden hut. In 1898 the railway replaced ponies and a summit café building was designed by Sir Clough Williams Ellis, the creator of Porthmeirion. In 2009 the latest building to crown the summit — Hafod Eryri — was opened.

Moel Siabod from Afon Llugwy

Moel Siabod

Pont Cyfyng – Llyn y Foel – Daear Ddu ridge – Moel Siabod – Coed Bryn-engan – Afon Llugwy – Pont Cyfyng

Distance/time: 10.5km / 6½ miles.

Start: A small car park beside Bryn Glo café on the A5 in Capel Curig.

Grid ref: SH 735 571

Summits: Moel Siabod

Ordnance Survey Map: Ordnance Survey Outdoor Leisure OL17 *Snowdon/Yr Wyddfa – Conwy Valley/Dyffryn Conwy*

Walk outline

A steady ascent on goods paths and farm tracks past old quarry workings to an impressive hanging valley. This is followed by pleasant, easy scrambling (or steep walking) up a fine rocky ridge in a superb setting. Easier options are always available. Descent is by the gentle northern slopes above Capel Curig with a return beside the wooded Afon Llugwy.

Moel Siabod

Moel Siabod is unusual in that it presents a gentle characterless face to the north saving its charms for the southern approach. As a result, the mountain is scarcely noticed from Capel Curig as all eyes are drawn by the Snowdon Horseshoe. By contrast, the shapely southern slopes are almost unrecognisable as the same mountain as they rise dramatically above Glyn Lledr — a fine pointed summit, a deeply-cut cwm with imposing headwall, and a rocky ridge leading directly to the summit.

Approaching Llyn y Foel

This route uses the approach from Capel Curig to reach the ridge, which provides a superb easy, escapable scramble almost from the shore of the lake to the summit. A perfect introduction to scrambling in Snowdonia. The wheatear loves high moorland, so keep your eyes open around Llyn y Foel and on the northern slopes of the mountain on the descent.

Wheatear

Summit view: *There are superb views north to the Glyderau and Tryfan*

The Walk

1. Turn right out of the car park and walk along the A5 towards **Capel Curig**. In about 200 metres turn left into a minor lane crossing **Afon Llugwy** by the old stone bridge (**Pont Cyfyng**). Walk along the lane to houses (about 100 metres), then bear right over a cattle grid and go ahead up a steep farm road signed to 'Moel Siabod'.

Where the road turns sharp right to the **farm** higher up, follow the signed footpath straight ahead. The footpath joins the farm track again. Bear left and continue the climb onto the high pastures with the pyramidal peak of Moel Siabod rising ahead.

2. Higher up, the path runs beside a **small lake**, then rises more steeply passing spoil heaps and **ruined miners' cottages**. Pass a small but deep **water-filled quarry** and rise to a broad saddle overlooking the secluded **Llyn y Foel** below the impressive headwall of the cwm. The **Daear Ddu ridge** can now be seen for the first time rising from the far side of the lake.

3. The most direct route to the base of the ridge is straight ahead keeping to the right of the lake, but for better views of the cwm and the ridge, bear left around the lake passing over the outflow. For the best scrambling keep to the right-hand side of the ridge almost overlooking the cwm. Any difficulties can be turned on the left and easier ground can always be reached by moving left. *It is also possible to avoid the scrambling altogether by following the footpath well over to the left. The ridge leads directly to* **the summit**.

Views from the summit are wide in clear conditions, especially the dramatic view west into the Snowdon Horseshoe. To the north stand the rounded backs of the Glyderau and Carneddau, with Tryfan peeping over the ridge. To the south you have the dramatic fall to Llyn y Foel, with the hills of southern Snowdonia stretching out beyond the woods of Glyn Lledr.

4. To descend, walk back along the summit ridge. The Capel Curig path leaves the ridge about halfway along (immediately before the rocky section) and heads north (left) to pass through the woods of **Coed Bryn-engan**.

5. In the lower section of the woods at a prominent T-junction turn right and follow the forest road to eventually walk beside **Afon Llugwy**. A good path then stays beside the river passing through two grazing fields to reach the lane by the bridge — **Pont Cyfyng** to complete the walk. ♦

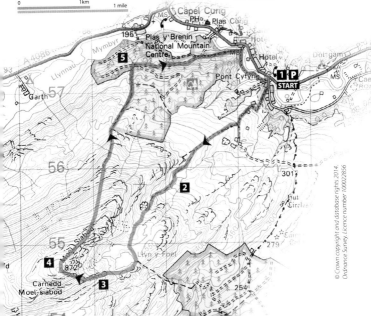

Moel Hebog from the Beddgelert Forest

Moel Hebog

*Beddgelert – Moel Hebog – Moel yr Ogof – Moel Lefn –
Beddgelert Forest – Lon Gwyfrai – Beddgelert*

Distance/time: 12km/7½ miles

Start: The village of Beddgelert. Car parks fill early in the summer season. Begin the walk at the National Park car park near the TIC

Grid ref: SH 588 481

Summits: Moel Hebog, Moel yr Ogof & Moel Lefn

Ordnance Survey Map: Ordnance Survey Outdoor Leisure OL17 *Snowdon/Yr Wyddfa – Conwy Valley/Dyffryn Conwy*

Walk outline

A steep, direct ascent of Moel Hebog's classic northeast ridge is followed by an elevated walk along the broad switchback ridge connecting it to the minor summits of Moel yr Ogof and Moel Lefn. Return is made by the forest paths and tracks of the Beddgelert Forest using part of the recently created Lon Gwyfrai cycleway and leisure trail.

Moel Hebog

Any mountain standing in Snowdon's shadow should be completely overwhelmed by it — not so Moel Hebog. Rising immediately to the west of Beddgelert and with Snowdon safely out of sight behind Yr Aran, it completely dominates the village. It is seen at its best on the descent from Rhyd-Ddu to Beddgelert against a foreground of the conifers of the Beddgelert Forest.

This route takes the classic direct ascent from Beddgelert and then continues north along the rounded ridge over the smaller summits of Moel Ogof and Moel Lefn, with a return through the beautiful woods of the Beddgelert Forest. There are several boggy hollows along the ridge where you will see the fleecy heads of cotton grass swaying in the breeze.

Moel yr Ogof

Cotton grass

The Walk

1. Leave the car park by the signed exit beside the information board and take the path on the right to walk beside the **Welsh Highland Railway**. The path soon passes under a railway bridge, then swings right to reach a T-junction with a lane. Turn left and follow the lane beside a tumbling stream, crossing the railway twice, to reach a farmhouse ('**Cwm Cloch Canol**') immediately before the track turns sharp left.

2. Turn right through a gate opposite the farmhouse and follow the recently created cycleway and footpath — **Lon Gwyrfai**.

In around 150 metres the **Moel Hebog** path splits left across the open pasture, before rising steeply onto the northeast ridge of the mountain. Ascend the ridge until the angle eases as you approach the crags at the head of the impressive **Cwm Bleiddiaid** (*'hollow of the wolves'*).

3. From here the path bends left to avoid the crags, then turns right-wards up the scree-covered upper slopes of the mountain to a subsidiary top at the head of the crags. The **summit** is an easy, short walk to the south.

4. From the summit descend northwest beside the wall to **Bwlch Meillionen**. From here ascend directly through a cleft in the crags above, passing an area of pools to reach the next summit — **Moel yr Ogof** (*'hill of the cave',* *said to have once been the* *hideout of Owain Glyndŵr*).

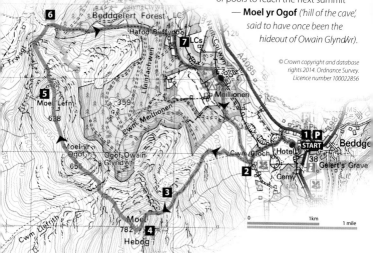

Mountain pools: *Pools on the broad ridge near the summit of Moel yr Ogof*

Continue northwest to the next top, **Moel Lefn**, a straightforward 1 kilometre /¾ mile walk along the rounded ridge crossing a fence partway at its junction with an old stone wall.

5. From Moel Lefn continue north to a small saddle — **Bwlch Sais**, *(the Englishman's pass)*. The path continues the descent to pass a tiny quarry on the right with a wall ahead. Cross the fence where it joins the wall and follow

the path left down beside the wall to a larger saddle — **Bwlch Cwm-trwsgl**.

6. A stile on the right here leads into the woods of the **Beddgelert Forest**. Now for the complicated route finding! Cross the stile and enter the trees. Descend a rocky and often wet path to a forest road. Turn left here and after 100 metres or so, look for a narrow, but well-used footpath on the right. Follow this path through the trees keeping right at a fork to enter a **large clearing** by a gap in the wall. Follow the obvious traversing path (marked by well spaced blue posts)

Wide skies: *Distant views of the Snowdon group are visible for much of the walk set agains a foreground of conifers*

straight ahead with superb views to Snowdon. Ignore a path on the left.

A stile in the fence ahead takes you back into the woods again. Follow the path to a forest road, turn left, then after a few metres turn right onto a narrow footpath which takes you directly down the hillside crossing a number of forest roads again. Keep descending to pass through a gate in a wall out of the trees.

7. The path now leads through a small rough field with a cottage ('**Hafod Ruffydd Uchaf**') on the right. Walk down the field edge, passing the cottage, to a stile that leads onto a forest road.

Turn right along the forest road. Ignore tracks off to the right and in 350 metres, just as the forest road bends left, take a surfaced path on the right which soon crosses the river by an **old stone bridge**. The path continues down through the woods to a T-junction with a forest road. Turn left and follow the forest road down to a railway crossing with the **Meillionen Forest Campsite** beyond.

Turn right just before the crossing,

signed 'Beddgelert 2.5km'. The path runs beside the railway now. At a fork keep right ('Beddgelert') and at a second fork bear left down to cross a **wooden footbridge** over the stream.

Go through a gate beyond the bridge and follow the gravel path back to the farmhouse of 'Cwm Cloch Canol'. Turn left down the access road and retrace the outward route back to Beddgelert. ♦

The Welsh Highland Railway

The Welsh Highland Railway has been described as 'one of the greatest white elephants of Wales's industrial history'. It was opened in 1922, but after just 15 troubled years it closed in 1937. The trackbed deteriorated over the years until it was renovated in four phases between 1997 and 2011. The Ffestiniog & Welsh Highland Railways were voted North Wales' top attraction in the 2013 National Tourism Awards.

Rhinog Fawr from Gloyw Lyn

Rhinog Fawr

Cwm Bychan – Roman Steps – Llyn Du – Rhinog Fawr – Glyow Lyn – Llyn Bychan

Distance/time: 8km / 5 miles

Start: Small car park at the head of Cwm Bychan immediately beyond the lake. A small fee is charged

Grid ref: SH 645 314

Summits: Rhinog Fawr

Ordnance Survey Map: Ordnance Survey Outdoor Leisure OL18 Harlech, *Porthmadog & Bala/Y Bala*

Walk outline

Easy walking on an ancient stone-paved trackway takes you into the heart of the Rhinog. From the saddle a narrow path weaves between heather and rocks past the sheltered Llyn Du and up the mountain's northern slopes to the summit. Return is made by a more exploratory route through typical Rhinog heather and rocks by Gloyw Lyn to rejoin the outward route.

The Rhinogydd

Although the majority of walkers will have first become aware of the Rhinog hills from their striking outline seen from the east, often against a glorious sunset, there is little doubt that the best approach is from the west along the sinuous lane which leaves Llanbedr to rise beside the tumbling Afon Artro beneath a canopy of ancient oaks. At the head of the lane the sheltered Llyn Cwm Bychan comes as a pleasant surprise and at the same time a slight disappointment as the main summits fall out of view.

This route uses the famous Roman Steps to approach Rhinog Fawr with a return by the beautiful Gloyw Lyn — a perfect finish on a golden evening. The Rhinog hills are famous for the feral goats that thrive in this land of heather and rock.

Rhinog heather

Feral goats

The Walk

1. Go through the gate at the top of the car park and turn right onto the well-made path which crosses the **stream** and soon enters **oak woods**. After the woods, cross a small **stone bridge** and continue the ascent on the famous paved path known as 'Roman Steps'.

The steps — almost 500 in all — look recently laid and are of unknown date, but certainly not Roman. This route through the hills is of great antiquity though and had probably been in use for several centuries before being paved. The steps are most likely of medieval origin and their purpose will quickly become apparent to anyone who wanders off-route.

2. Follow the path to the highest point of the pass, known as **Bwlch Tyddiad**.

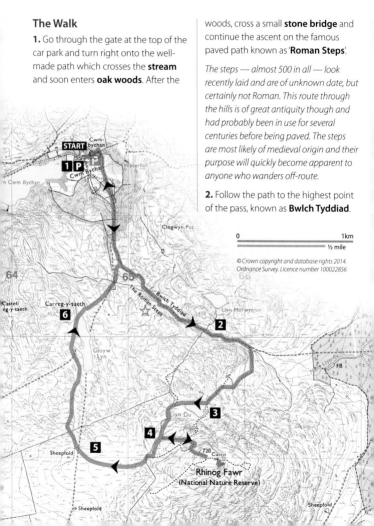

© Crown copyright and database rights 2014.
Ordnance Survey. Licence number 100022856

Wild land: *The view north from the summit of Rhinog Fawr*

Continue ahead descending towards the conifer plantations which sprawl across the eastern slopes of the mountain. About 300 metres beyond the highest point, and immediately before a **wall** on the right which emerges from the heather and then swings away down the valley, bear right onto a narrow footpath which crosses the wall then rises to the picturesque little lake of **Llyn Du** (*black lake*).

3. Follow the path along the right-hand shore scrambling over boulders to reach a **well-built stone wall** about 150 metres beyond the lake.

The path now heads left up beside the wall until the way is blocked by a small rock face. Turn right through a gap in the wall here and stay on the path which more or less follows the wall.

4. Stay with the path and the wall to reach a distinct level area carpeted in marshy grass just before the wall begins to descend. Immediately before this, take the path left up the final rocky slopes of the mountain. A little higher,

Mountain lake: *Gloyw Llyn sits in a beautiful location high up below Rhinog Fawr*

where the path appears to level, bear right and make a final steep climb to the **summit**.

Here at the centre of the Rhinog the views are stunning in all directions — north across the rocky wilds of Moel Morwynion to Clip with the peaks of northern Snowdonia beyond, and south to Rhinog Fach, Y Llethr and Diffwys.

To descend, retrace your steps down to the level marshy area by the wall.

Go left here by the wall for about 200 metres or so. The wall is no longer visible but a narrow footpath on the right takes you back to it. Go through a gap in the wall and turn left beside it for about 100 metres to a point where it veers left. Take the vague path ahead (west) from here which soon swings rightwards (northwest) through the heather. At an obvious crossing path go left and follow it on a contouring line with **Gloyw Lyn** visible below.

5. Shortly, the path passes above a wide gully on the right, its right-hand side composed of flat slabby rocks. At the bottom of the gully there is a stone wall crossed by a ladder stile. Soon, the path swings right down to this stile.

Cross the stile and follow the good path which heads left for a few metres before it swings right and then heads directly down towards Gloyw Lyn. Take the path along the left-hand side of the lake.

6. At the end of the lake a **fisherman's path** weaves down through the bracken and swings right to rejoin the outgoing route below Roman Steps. Turn left here to return to the car park. ♦

Roman Steps

Access to Rhinog Fawr from the north is via Bwlch Tyddiad, an ancient pass through the hills which has been in use for millennia. The highest, roughest parts of the pass are stone paved and are known locally as 'Roman Steps'. Despite the name and the antiquity of the route, the steps are not Roman. They are in fact the well preserved remains of a medieval packhorse trail leading from Chester to Harlech Castle.

Aran Benllyn and Aran Fawddwy from Bala Lake/Llyn Tegid

The **Arans**

Cwm Cywarch – Hengwm – Drysgol – Aran Fawddwy –
Aran Benllyn – Aran Fawddwy – Blaencywarch

Distance/time: 18km/11¼ miles

Start: There is parking available on a large stretch of open common land near the end of the lane in Cwm Cywarch

Grid ref: SH 853 185

Summits: Aran Fawddwy, Aran Benllyn & Gwaun y Llwyni

Ordnance Survey Map: Ordnance Survey Outdoor Leisure OL32 *Cadair Idris & Llyn Tegid*

Walk outline

From the impressive head of Cwm Cywarch a steady climb up an impressive cwm takes you onto the rounded shoulders of the Aran ridge where a sweeping grass ridge leads onto the rocky summit plateau. Almost level out-and-back walking allows you to bag both summits before a long, damp walk over moors is followed by a steep descent beside Craig Cywarch.

The Arans

Often overlooked in favour of their more famous and impressive neighbour, Cadair Idris, the Aran hills remain unjustifiably neglected. Even the impressive sight of Aran Benllyn rising above Bala Lake seems to entice few to venture into these hills. Cwm Cywarch offers a superb approach to the two highest summits in the group where the towering, castellated buttresses of Craig Cywarch present one of the most impressive sights in southern Snowdonia. It is remarkable that this area is so little visited.

Above Hengwm

This walk uses the long northern arm of Aran Benllyn to gain the main ridge from where both the high tops can be accessed with a return by the beautiful Cwm Croes. Red grouse are common on the heather moors of the Arans and neighbouring Berwyns.

Red grouse

The Walk

1. From the parking area continue along the lane towards the **farms** at the valley head and in about 300 metres turn right over a footbridge signed 'Aran Benllyn and Aran Fawddwy'. The path is enclosed by walls at first, then rises diagonally up the open slopes of **Pen yr Allt Uchaf**, with impressive views back to Craig Cywarch.

2. Where the angle eases on the broad flat shoulder of the mountain, bear left up the rounded grass ridge parallel to the fence. Cross a stile on the skyline at the top of the rise (**Drysgol**) and walk along the gentle grass ridge with good views right to the craggy eastern face of the two Aran giants. At the **memorial cairn** there are equally impressive views back down the sweeping **Hengwm** towards Craig Cywarch.

(**Gwaun y Llwyni**, seen so impressively from Hengwm, can be included by an out-and-back walk southwest along the ridge from here.)

Secret lake: *Aran Fawddwy and Craiglyn Dyfi, the source of Afon Dyfi*

3. The path heads northwest now along the edge of the cwm to cross a stile below the final rocky slopes of **Aran Fawddwy**. A faint path leads through the jumbled boulders to a sub top at GR. 860 221. From here it is a short amble northeast across the stony plateau — reminiscent of the Glyderau — to Aran Fawddwy.

(In good conditions it is worth the additional 1.5 kilometres/1 mile to **Aran Benllyn**, for its superb views north across Bala Lake [Llyn Tegid].)

4. From **Aran Fawddwy** return to the subsidiary top, then head southwest to cross a stile in the fence ahead (ignore a stile on the right). Follow the footpath beside the fence which becomes better established as you descend. Things get pretty wet in parts but **board walks** take you over the worst sections.

5. Continue to the lowest point on the moors ahead before the ground rears up to the bulky mass of **Glasgwm** (just over 3 kilometres/2 miles from Aran Fawddwy). There is a **small reedy pool** here almost on the watershed. Turn left on a footpath which soon follows the stream down beside the towering crags of **Craig Cywarch**.

6. In about 1.5 kilometres/1 mile, join a track near a small cottage over to the left ('**Bryn Hafod**') and go right passing a farm ('**Blaencywarch**') to join the lane. Follow the lane back to the parking area to complete the route. ◆

Craig Cau dominates the dark Llyn Cau

Cadair Idris

Minffordd – Llyn Cau – Mynydd Pencoed – Craig Cau –
Penygadair (Cadair Idris) – Mynydd Moel – Nant Cadair

Distance/time: 9.5km / 6 miles

Start: The National Park car park at Dôl Idris, located just off the junction of the A487 and the B4405l

Grid ref: SH 732 115

Summits: Mynydd Pencoed, Penygadair & Mynydd Moel

Ordnance Survey Map: Ordnance Survey Outdoor Leisure OL32 *Cadair Idris & Llyn Tegid*

Walk outline

Steep walking on a good path through a wooded gorge leads to the impressive mountain lake of Llyn Cau enclosed by the dark vegetated crags of Craig Cau. A fine ridge walk around the rim of the cwm leads over Mynydd Pencoed and on to Cadair's highest point — Penygadair. Easy walking along the summit plateau to the subsidiary summit of Mynydd Moel, followed by a steep descent over rounded slopes to rejoin the outward route in the wooded gorge.

Cadair Idris

There is little doubt that the most memorable view of Cadair Idris is from the north, either across the broad sand flats of the Mawddach estuary, or the calm waters of Llynnau Cregennen below the northern cliffs of Tyrrau Mawr. From the south the mountain is rather featureless and has far less impact, but concealed in these softer folds is the most impressive mountain cwm south of Snowdon.

Views to Cardigan Bay

This route follows the classic round of Cwm Cau, a superb ridge walk in spectacular surroundings and undoubtedly the best route on the mountain. The red kite is an increasingly common sight in Southern Snowdonia, identifiable by its distinctive 'forked' tail.

Red kite

The Walk

1. Go through the gate at the back of the car park by the information board and turn right along an avenue of trees. Cross the bridge and soon pass in front of the '**Ystradlyn Visitor Centre**'. After the footbridge, turn right through a gate into the nature reserve to begin

the stiff pull up through woods beside the tumbling **Nant Cadair** stream over to the right.

2. As you emerge from the woods the path soon bends left towards the enclosed lake of **Llyn Cau** which remains out of view until you are almost at the water's edge.

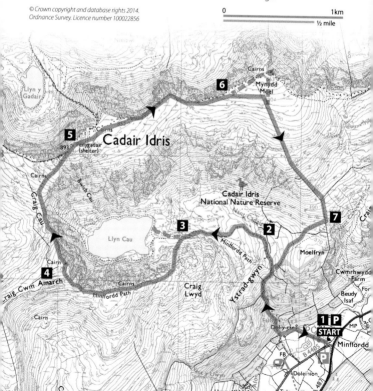

Sea view: *Cadair's position close to the sea offers grand views across Cyfrwy and Tyrrau Mawr to Cardigan Bay*

3. On the lip of the cwm the path splits — the path ahead leads down to the shore of the lake with the path to the left rising up towards the ridge.

It is worth the short detour to the edge of the lake for the stunning view of Craig Cau towering above the dark water, but you will need to return to this junction and take the left fork to continue.

As you gain the ridge you are treated

to fine views southwards across to the Tarren hills and beyond. Follow the path along the edge of **Craig Cau** to the subsidiary top of **Mynydd Pencoed** perched on the very edge of the huge cliffs overhanging the lake (take care in poor visibility!).

4. From Mynydd Pencoed make a short descent due north to the saddle separating Craig Cau from Penygadair. From here a short, stiff pull takes you onto the summit slopes and finally **Penygadair**, Cadair's highest point.

In clear conditions the view out over the

Mountain lake: *Llyn y Gadair nestles in the huge glacial hollow below the north face of the mountain*

Mawddach estuary and across Cardigan Bay to the distant hills of the Lleyn Peninsula is magnificent, particularly late in the day with the promise of a fine sunset. With reasonable clarity the entire curve of Cardigan Bay should be visible from Bardsey (Ynys Enlli) to the tip of Pembrokeshire.

The small ruined shelter on the summit is said to have once been used to offer refreshments to those making the ascent on pony from Tŷ Nant.

5. From the **summit**, head east across the broad summit plateau towards **Mynydd Moel**, just over 1 kilometre/¾ mile away.

6. As the ground begins the gentle rise to Mynydd Moel, either continue to the summit, or, if you want to miss out this minor summit, take the contouring path that breaks away to the right. Eventually a wall is either reached or is visible down to the right. Head for this and descend steeply on its left-hand side.

Alternatively, from the summit of Mynydd Moel reach the wall by a direct descent south-southeast.

7. Follow the wall to a stile (in about 1 kilometre/¾ mile) on the right. Cross the

wall here and head down rightwards to cross the stream (**Nant Cadair**) by a footbridge near the point where the Minffordd Path (used earlier) emerges from the woods.

Turn left here and retrace the outward route down through the woods beside the stream and Ystradlyn Visitor Centre to complete the walk . ♦

The 'Chair of Idris'

Cadair Idris means 'Chair of Idris', Idris being a personal name. The most likely candidate is Idris ap Gwyddno a prince of Meirionydd who won a battle on the mountain. Irdis was also known as 'Idris Gawr' — the Great or 'Giant'. This could be the origin of the legend that claims Cadair Idris to be the 'chair of the giant Idris. Chair in this context could also be taken as referring to the 'seat' or 'stronghold of Idris'.

Useful Information

Visit Wales

The Visit Wales website covers everything from accommodation and events to attractions and adventure. For information on the area covered by this book, see: **www.visitwales.co.uk**

Snowdonia National Park

The Snowdonia National Park website also has information on things to see and do, plus maps, webcams and news. **www.snowdonia-npa.gov.uk**

Tourist Information Centres

The main TICs provide free information on everything from accommodation and travel to what's on and walking advice.

Betws-y-coed	01690 710426	TIC.BYC@eryri-npa.gov.uk
Beddgelert	01766 890615	TIC.Beddgelert@eryri-npa.gov.uk
Harlech	01766 780658	TIC.Harlech@eryri-npa.gov.uk
Dolgellau	01341 422888	TIC.Dolgellau@eryri-npa.gov.uk
Aberdyfi	01654 767321	TIC.Aberdyfi@eryri-npa.gov.uk

Emergencies

Snowdonia is covered by volunteer mountain rescue teams. In a real emergency:

1. Make a note of your location (with OS grid reference, if possible); the name, age and sex of the casualty; their injuries; how many people are in the group; and your mobile phone number.

2. Call 999 or 112 and ask for the North Wales police, and then for Mountain Rescue.

3. Give them your prepared details.

4. Do NOT change position until contacted by the mountain rescue team.

Weather

The Met Office operates a 24 hour online weather forecast

Follow the link from the National Park website **www.eryri-npa.gov.uk/visiting/your-weather-forecast-service** or see www.metoffice.gov.uk